The Trouble-Making Finch

Other Works by Len Roberts

Poetry
Cohoes Theater
From the Dark
Sweet Ones
Black Wings
Learning about the Heart (chapbook)
Dangerous Angels
The Million Branches (chapbook)
Counting the Black Angels

Translations from the Hungarian
Selected Poems of Sándor Csoóri
Call to Me in My Mother Tongue (chapbook)

The Trouble-Making Finch

POEMS BY LEN ROBERTS

University of Illinois Press
Urbana and Chicago

Library of Congress Cataloging-in-Publication Data

Roberts, Len, 1947–
The trouble-making finch : poems / by Len Roberts.
p.   cm.
ISBN 0-252-06693-6 (pbk. : alk. paper)
I. Title.
PS3568.O2389T76   1998
811'.54—dc21 97-21189
CIP

Digitally reprinted from the first paperback printing

073004

Acknowledgments

My thanks to the editors of the following journals in which some of these poems, in various versions, first appeared:

The American Poetry Review: "Acupuncture and Cleansing at Forty-Eight"; "And where were you"; "518"; "God's Blessing"; "Silence on the Day My Father Was Carried Away"; "Sister Ann Zita Shows Us the Foolishness of the Forbidden Books"; "Snapper, Wassergass"; and "The Trouble-Making Finch"

Atlanta Review: "My son won't stop making"

Boulevard: "The Flying Monk in Flames" and "Noon, Wednesday in Wassergass"

Christian Science Monitor: "In Cursive"

Cream City Review: "The Stone"

Georgia Review: "We Were Insects and Animals"

Green Mountains Review: "Climbing the Three Hills in Search of the Best Christmas Tree"

Jeopardy: "Tapping in the Seed"

The Journal: "Taking Inventory as She Weeds"

Many Mountains Moving: "Doing the Laundry"; "The Long Ride Home"; and "A shoe in the road, autumn's"

New England Review: "Obedient" and "Thinning the Walnuts"

Passages North: "Terrible Angels"

Poet Lore: "Ripping slate off the barn roof,"

Poetry East: "Nailing in New Braces"

Poetry Northwest: "Angels in the Experimental Catechism/Math Class"; "Anointing Her Five Senses"; "The Burning Hours"; "Correcting the Lisp"; and "Last night, between dusk and"

Quarterly West: "All day cutting wood, thinking," and "Contem-

plating Again the Jade Chrysanthemum; or, Why the Ancient
Chinese Poets Remained Unmarried"

The Southern Review: "The Equation"

West Branch: "Sister Ann Zita Shows Us the Foolishness of the
Forbidden Books"

Willow Springs: "Double Yolk"

World Poetry (http://www.worldpoetry.com): "Acupuncture and
Cleansing at Forty-Eight"; "Contemplating Again the Jade Chry-
santhemum; or, Why the Ancient Chinese Poets Remained Un-
married"; "God's Blessing"; "Noon, Wednesday in Wassergass";
and "Sister Ann Zita Shows Us the Foolishness of the Forbidden
Books"

"Acupuncture and Cleansing at Forty-Eight" and "Correcting the
Lisp" from *Identity Lessons: Learning American Style: An Anthol-
ogy of Contemporary Writing,* edited by Maria Mazziotti Gillan and
Jennifer Gillan. Copyright Len Roberts, 1996. Used by arrangement
with Penguin Books, a member of Penguin Putnam Inc.

My thanks to Yaddo, for their residence grants that gave me the
peace and quiet to write, and to Nancy, for her patience and under-
standing. I am especially indebted to Larry Lieberman and Steve
Berg for their insightful, caring, and always constructive comments
about so many of these poems.

For Philip Levine and Gerald Stern

Contents

Part 1

Acupuncture and Cleansing at Forty-Eight

No longer eating meat or dairy
        products or refined sugar,
I lie on the acupuncturist's
        mat stuck with twenty
needles and know a little how
Saint Sebastian felt with those
        arrows
piercing him all over, his poster
tacked to the wall before my fourth-
        grade desk
as I bent over the addition and loss,
tried to find and name the five oceans,
        seven continents,
drops of blood with small windows of
        light strung
from each of his wounds, blood like
the blood on my mother's pad the day
        she hung
it before my face and said I was making
        her bleed to death,
blood like my brother's that day
he hung from the spiked barb
at the top of the fence,
a railroad track of stitches gleaming
for years on the soft inside of his arm,
blood like today when Dr. Ming extracts
        a needle and dabs

a speck of red away, one from my eyelid,
   one from my cheek,
the needles trying to open my channels
   of *chi*
so I can sleep at night without choking,
so I don't have to fear waking my wife
   hawking the hardened mucus out,
so I don't have to lie there thinking
of those I hate, of those who have died,
   the needles
tapped into the kidney point, where
   memories reside,
tapped into the liver point, where
   poisons collect,
into the feet and hands, the three
   chakra of the chest
that split the body in half, my right
   healthy, my left in pain,
my old friend's betrayal lumped in my
   neck,
my old love walking away thirty years
   ago
stuck in my lower back, father's death,
   mother's
lovelessness lodged in so many parts
it may takes years, Dr. Ming whispers,
   to wash them out,
telling me to breathe deep, to breathe
   hard,
the body is nothing but a map of the
   heart.

You were
waking me on the cold seat
   of the great-winged
DeSoto at the Cohoes Drive-In,
that worried look on your face
telling me we were late,
   past two,
Sean Connery thunderballing
   his way
out of Russia, near the end
   of the show.
Now he's seventy-two.
Now you're nearly forty-eight.
I have a daughter graduated
   from law school,
your age when I last saw you
   burning
letters in the old barrel
on your winter driveway,
shouting at me not to come back
   if I left,
your blue bathrobe whipped
up by the wind to show your
long, smooth, tanned legs.
I've kept in touch with friends
   of friends,
your telephone number hidden
   somewhere

now even I can't remember, with
your red and white checked summer
    cotton dress
crumpling in a pile as you stepped
    out of it,
and the 36C black bra,
the purplish-black mascara
those many times you wept,
me always trying to take off your silk
    underpants,
you always holding back,
masturbating me OK, sucking on me OK,
but never the whole way, except that
    once
on my maiden aunt's couch, time
    grown dim
to me now as your telephone number
that had a five and a one and an eight
with four other digits completely blank.

Silence on the Day My Father Was Carried Away

When I read that the angels flew
     down
on the appointed day to wrap the
     dead
in their arms and carry them away,
I thought of my father hugging
     Jeannine
or Irene or fat Annette
on his piss-stained sheets,
how they'd roll and laugh, riffs
from his harmonica drifting out,
sometimes a groan, a slap, a shout,
sometimes nothing but silence,
where I find myself today, cold March,
staring at the two ducks on the pond
who keep returning, their ripples widening
across the entire surface half acre,
my mind trying to explain where
my wife has been these last few hours,
if she'll come home from shopping
     with nothing again,
how I'll stare at her lips
to see if the lipstick is smeared,
how I'll look, when she turns,
at the wrinkles of her blouse,
the lint on her sweater,
hearing the words we'll mutter

in the dim kitchen as we circle
     the table,
picking up mail to peer at labels,
     clattering
the plates, forks, knives, and spoons
down onto the blank blue placemats
we'd bought years ago, four
for a dollar, I'll remind her,
     nodding
as though there were nothing more
     important.

The Equation

Twenty-six years dead
and still you stir
my sleep, wake
me at 4 A.M.
the entire week
before your final date,
point me to sit
and learn the assigned
words, commit
to memory the capitals
and states,

   the value of x
always bringing you
hovering, close, your
beer breath in my breath
as you bent to trace
the known and unknown,
as though

   that might explain
why the woman had left
or the other son's death,
how you had come to weigh
105 beer-soaked pounds at
the end, a stick figure
of a man bent over a sheet
of scratchings you tried
desperately to show me
made some kind of sense,

whispering in that hushed
voice I hear as clearly
now as I did then
to pay attention
to the equal sign,
that what is given
is given is given.

Tapping in the Seed

With each seed dropped in
I renounced Satan and His sins,
crawling behind my grandmother
like a creeper vine
as we made our way down
board-edged lines
of planned cucumbers
and radishes and lettuce,
a bead of her spit dripped
with each seed before
she covered it with
In the name of the Lord
and a *Satan begone*
for good measure, the
small crucifixes strung
with wire to the rusted
fence, the glowing faces
of saints peeping from
the staked tomato plants,
my grandmother's thick
finger now and then
tapping my forehead hard
the way she tapped
the seeds deeply in,
telling me evil
was never far behind,
look at what
my mother and father did,

dirt crumbling into my eyes
even as she whispered
that I was born in sin,
grown slanted like a tree
planted in a strong wind,
her farmers' hands nearly
knocking me over as she leaned
me across the still unplanted
rows and commanded me to *straighten
up, straighten up*, the muscles
in my back tight as she held me
firm beneath that brilliant sun,
one hand grasping air, the other
sinking into the furrowed earth.

Contemplating Again the Jade Chrysanthemum; or, Why the Ancient Chinese Poets Remained Unmarried

Cast out of the house again,
    fuming
at my wife, my teenaged son
who has come back from his previous
    life
barely disguised as a pig who drops
    underwear,
socks, books, video games anywhere,
I keep repeating it's no wonder
the ancient Chinese poets remained
    unmarried
during their walks
of Ten Thousand Miles
and river rides
of Ten Thousand Sorrows.
I try to imagine Tu Fu watching
    Kung Sung
dance with two swords, teaching
him the black art of calligraphy
with a wife jabbing him in the ribs,
whispering for him to keep his eyes
    to home, she knows
he is not contemplating the jade chrysanthemum
or the deep heart of the emerald,
he's not kidding anyone,
or Li Po raising his cracked blue jug
to the moon while his cracked boy blasts
another monster-rock video three rooms
    away,

or Po Chu-i driven to chew ferns
because he couldn't balance the budget,
or Emperor Wu of the Han listening
  to tales
of the spirit world, trying to prolong
his life despite his children's tuition
  being due,
me fingering a list of a hundred chores
  to do this spring
as I watch smoke rise from the chimney
a good half mile down there,
  serpent
coiled with tail in mouth a few
  seconds above our house
before the north wind from the hill
  blows it apart.

Mission, Late March, 1960

On a night like this my brother
and I would roam Main and Remsen,
knocking over cardboard boxes
the white-shirted managers
of J. C. Penney's and Woolworth's
dragged out before locking up,
the drugstores the best,
with their blue and yellow pills,
their plastic bags and vials,
long ribbons of gauze we'd bandage
ourselves with and limp to our room,
pockets full of contraband,
synchronizing our watches
in the dark of late March, 1960,
my brother soon off to Vietnam
only to return to twenty-seven years
of little steps in the Albany
V.A. Hospital's green corridors.
Look at us as we mount the stairs
with clumped feet and stumps
for hands. Try to see our eyes
wrapped tight behind layers
that will not let in a single ray
of light. We've swallowed
all the pills and gone back for more,
we've outrun a police car,
an old man with a cane,
and one shooting star that flashed

over Desormau's Packing Plant so brilliantly
we almost stopped, we almost took it for a sign,
but we had a mission to fulfill, a duty
to get back and write in secret code
everything we saw, everything we knew.

Snapper, Wassergass

Nights now we wait for his return,
my boy and I sitting on the blue
    front porch,
whispering about the horned curve
of his beak, the way he hung
on to the garbage can lid
as I lifted his good fifty pounds
and whirled and swung but still
he did not let go as he flew
the twenty feet back to our lawn.
I wanted to cram the rifle muzzle
    down his throat,
blow him completely apart,
my son wailed to put him in the trunk
    of the car,
drop him off at the reservoir,
his departing hiss at me a warning
I did not take lightly,
having seen those eyes before,
and that thick shell,
that reptile brain,
knowing even as I let him go
that he would be back again.

The Blacktop Act

Old Leo would turn his one good eye toward the shade
    and start to hum,
Fat Sam shuffle a little closer with his tamp held
    inches off the ground,
and then it would begin, the worst
part of working blacktop in 100-degree heat in
    Cohoes, New York—
"It's All in the Game" or "The Other Side of the Mountain,"
or Hank Williams sung with Canuck and Slovak twangs,
their two voices trembling above the can of oil
    we'd dip our shovels
and rakes in to keep the 'top from sticking and adding
    pounds to our work.
Now and then a car would stop, a window roll down,
and one of their friends shake his head
till the fumes drove him off or the heat crawled
    under his shirt
and he knew what it was like to be poor
    and hot and forced
to listen to the boss and the biggest man
    on the crew
destroy the words of any song they'd care enough
    to remember.
And they did care, Leo's rolling vowels,
Sam's clipped consonants belted out
with what breath they had left
even as one bent a cataracted eye to check
    that the line was straight,

even as one lifted the great fifteen-pound tamp
        and leveled
the humps the rest of us could not flatten.
With red bandannas around their necks
and straw hats strung tight about their heads,
they're shuffling their feet in a stiff dance,
a few inches right, a few inches left
while the 'top sizzles their soles
        and clings to their cuffs,
helping the day along until the sun grows
        too hot or
one of us gives up and sets his tool down
        to applaud,
making them bend that formal bow they'd practiced
        in cool dawn
while the trucks were warming up and the day
nothing but a promise of unending work.

The Trouble-Making Finch

A goldfinch is in
the juniper pfitzers,
raising hell for such
a bird-runt, branches
springing yesterday's
snows all over the place,
prisms arcing from his
small yellow wings,
his stirring orange feet,
and I see now this
troublemaker who
disturbs the noon-
day's stillness
is my father tap-
dancing on Boney's bar
until he stumbles
and falls off
into another
lover's arms,
her blue sweater
and tight black
slacks, a beehive of hair
that buzzes when he sets
a red carnation among
the strands, the finch
down there making a racket
worse than my father's
harmonica playing when

he was drunk, crumpling
into snowbanks on the way
home without losing a beat,
the tune an after-midnight
whine that made the neighbors
turn on their lights and
hang their heads from cold
windows to shout, *Shut up*
or *Turn it off*, the warbler
of Olmstead Street throwing
snowballs until the cops
would come and tuck him
into their car and take
him to his other home,
his absence then
startling
as the finch's when
I look down to curse
him again only to find
him gone, the small
wings and maddening beak,
the somersaulter
among needled twigs
who had disturbed my peace
and brought my dead father
back with his showing-off
zipping around and
foolishness,
his brief yellow streaks,
his fraction-of-an-ounce heart.

Part 2

All day cutting wood, thinking

of Han Shan boiling roots
for tea, of my father's head
circled with blue clouds of smoke,
wondering how many more years
I'll live, if I'll die as I've
dreamed, face up in a field,
not like my old man, hungover
on a Sunday morning that
suddenly turned into black
wings landing on his chest
and lifting him, a scene
I keep coming back to
even as I cut the wedge
of the black cherry that's
got a good three-foot diameter,
hope it'll fall the way it's
supposed to, trying to gauge
the wind, Han Shan repeating
*No way that can be followed
is the way,* leaving me with
the chain saw blowing blue
exhaust because the mix
grew a little rich when I got
to the bottom of the can,
wanting to cross myself
above the gravelly snarl
for my long-dead father,
for my living son, but

afraid to take my hand
off the saw, knowing all
too well it could kick
back and take part of my face,
bearing down until the first
creak comes and I scramble
through the bramble path
I'd cut a swath in earlier
to make my escape, every thought
gone except how fast that more-
than-eighty-foot tree would crash,
how much distance I could put
between me and it, knowing I
shouldn't, even as I do, look back.

Sister Ann Zita Shows Us the Foolishness of the Forbidden Books

The Plague of God, the Rod of God
Sister Ann Zita wrote on that clouded
    blackboard
while Donald Wilcox whispered
the Cock of God, the Cock of God
into Karen Awlen's red ear, making her
    lean forward,
her breasts shifting under the starched
    white blouse,
the silver dog on the silver chain dangling
    in that seventh-grade sunlight
as we all watched the Serpent of the
    Bottomless Pit
coil through the nine planets beneath which
Richie Freeman dunked strands of Donna's
    long gold hair into the inkwell,
Ann Harding and Ronny Michaels passing back
    and forth a note folded
at least ten times with *I love you* written
    in red at the crinkled center,
Al Aldon's fart so loud when he grabbed it mid-
    aisle
that Sister looked up from her Book of Devils
    and Stars to ask what was going on,
pointing to the demon with seven serpent heads,
    fourteen faces, and twelve wings,
telling us St. Paul said it would have been better
    if we had not been born

since we were all sinners, Donald whispering,
Yes, Yes, in the alley behind the Union Diner,
as he flapped his wings back there by the clothes closet
    till he fell
out of his seat, Sister reminding us it took Satan nine
    days, not a second,
to drop from Heaven to Hell, the hands of the big clock
    above the door
clicking toward twelve making me bend to tie my laces
    and see Barbara McGill
scratching her thigh, skirt hitched up to the mound
    of her ass,
the four lines her fingernails had raked a wavery blood
    red
through the short, yellow-white hairs, the bluish tint
    of her white, white skin.

Climbing the Three Hills in Search of the Best Christmas Tree

Just seven nights from the
    darkest
night of the year, my son
    and I climb
the three hills behind
    the white
house, his flashlight
    leaping
from hemlock to fir
    to white
pine and blue spruce
    and back
again. Up, up higher
    he runs,
shadow among larger
    shadows
in the below-zero,
    constellated,
half-mooned sky, his
    voice
so distant at times
    I think
it is the wind, a rustle
    of tall
grass, the squeak of my
    boots
on new snow, his silence
    making

me shout, *Where are you?*
    his floating
back, *Why are you so slow?*
    a good
question I ask myself to
    the beat
of my forty-eight-year-old
    heart,
so many answers rushing up
    that
I have to stop and command
    them back,
snow devils whirling
    before
me, behind me, on all
    sides,
names that gleam and
    black
out like ancient specks
    of moon-
light, that old track
    I step
onto like an escalator
    rising
to the ridge where the
    best
trees grow and I know
I will find my son.

And where were you

with your teepee and Lucky
    Strike
signals of smoke, when she
cornered me in the hallway,
cold as a rat she smashed
with the broom handle
till it broke and she began
with her small fists?
And when I disappeared under
    the bed,
behind the long black dress
    of the closet,
when I turned into words
at the kitchen table,
bologna, mischievous, fluorescent,
when I grew faster than the parti-
colored flash cards, a quotient,
    a divider,
a remainder, then a continent,
    yellow
Asia, brown Australia, mysterious
    blue
South America, and castanets clicked
    in my fingers
and my heart grew claws that scratched
    to get out,
where were you, wooden Indian deader
than the chief who stood outside
    Bernie's Cigar Shop

all nicked and scarred and scuffed
with just one good eye left to look out
on Ontario Street and the swirling ice-floed
	Mohawk River?
Where were you, dream catcher
	who floated
above my black bed with the red coal
	living
at the far end of your every breath,
my dark man, my ten crooked fingers
	with five rings
and five diamond chips, five gold
	initials
that told everyone but me you were
	just another drunk,
dirty hands on her white, white breasts,
dirty cock in her silk-satin cunt,
stupid half-breed who thought you could
	fuck
her white gloves and polka-dot dress
	and rows
of neat teeth and still be free
	to peddle bread
in your Golden Eagle truck's
eighty-miles-an-hour snowdrifted roads
	throughout the Adirondacks
where your grandfathers ate bark.
Dumb, long-dicked, alcoholic, pock-marked,
malarial-ridden, purple-hearted Indian,
	where
are you now I've grown big and strong
and am ready to bloody my hands with the bitch?

For my father, R.R.R., French-Mohawk,
long dead in Cohoes, New York

Ice Man, 1931

He had shoulders like Atlas
but instead of the world
my grandfather hauled
two-hundred-pound
blocks of ice up four
flights of stairs, one
hooked from each hand, then
down to the cobblestone
street again, the green
cart with brown horse again,
the click and giddyap
a few more doors down the block,
tipping his beret but bowing
to no one, the ice king
that long summer of upstate
New York, which lasted about
two months before the clouds
began to gather that would change his life.
That was 1931, the darkest hole
of the Depression, and though
I had not been born yet, I heard
each door he opened and closed,
the sound of coins clinking
in his workman's pockets —
I saw him spread sawdust
on the cart well before dawn,
and all over the air-blue cubes
that reflected not only the sky

but Cohoes Manufacturing
and the old ladies who trembled
on their porches for the cold
promise he would bring.
With each stop I watched
him scratch small, precise jottings
in the marbled composition book—
the numbers of days and blocks,
the hours of freezing and melting
added up and subtracted
those mornings I rode on top
of the always-shifting cargo,
when I brandished my icicle-dagger
and called down the avenging angels—
for I am the one who knows
he'll die in ten years
in a steaming Pacific jungle,
I am the one who knows
he'll sip rust-water from his rifle's bolt.
Here, I whispered with each bump
on each cobble, holding out the ice
that had already begun to melt,
Here, and *Here,* while
even the crows cheered me on
and the man with broad shoulders
and beret took whatever I offered,
looking back whenever I spoke
although he could not hear me or see me
as he lifted yet another chunk of ice
and cracked it between his teeth,
gnawing and licking the jagged edges
till they were tongue smooth and gleamed.

Double Yolk

Two yolks meant she'd get
      pregnant,
blood slipping around
      in the pan
like rivulets through
      clear mucus,
that's what I remember
as I stare at the blank blue plate,
think of how hungry I am,
of the Polish bread with bits
of fruit that stuck in my teeth
more than thirty years ago when
I'd spread my girlfriend's long,
tanned legs to lick her morning cream,
my mother's voice asking from the stove
if I want it anyway, now that I'm fifty
      and my three kids are grown,
asking if she should throw it in the trash can,
that sign, that flash in the pan
that had made my first love stop in the back
seat of the Chevy on Power Plant Road,
my mother's voice coming
through the green wool blanket
we'd tossed over our naked bodies,
over her perfume, my aftershave
      scent,
over our twenty-year-old hearts
      and asses and lips,

my mother asking if I want lots
        of pepper and salt,
if I want buttered toast with jam,
the two of us alone in her new
        apartment
of the Elderly Home, whiffs
of bacon drifting across,
a surprise, she whispers,
as she slides it all onto my plate.

In Cursive

I struggled with the *O*'s
touching the bottom and top
blue lines, their oval
flows, their short pig
tails that looped into
other *O*'s until the page
was filled and I turned
to the just-as-difficult
Q's, the day never ending
in that second-grade class
when we learned to write
in cursive *Mary saw John*,
and *Mary and John saw Spot*,
the picture of a dog
running down a street
littered with leaves

bringing me here to
October Wassergass
where my son rolls
in piles of reds, golds,
and yellows as his dog,
Magic, barks and barks,
the wind with its *W*'s
whispering over us
through the bare trees
that look like crooked
Y's and bent *T*'s, the

uncut grass of the field
a mess of *I*'s gone wild
on a page I conjure up
with its own margins
of *Good, Good, Good,*
and rows of glittering
stars on top, the world
like a bowl of alphabet
soup to be deciphered
and arranged while
the adults endlessly
talked and clattered
forks, knives, spoons,
the meanings there in
deep red sauce,
                                here
everywhere I look, the
letters arranging themselves
in *V*'s of geese flying south
and termite tracks carved
on undersides of bark,
even the leaves falling
a hieroglyph I strain
to make out, the instant
H and *A* and *N*, the split
second of perfect sense
before it's torn to shreds.

Correcting the Lisp

With five marbles in my mouth
I began with Thou Shalt,
    Thou Shalt Not,
reading for three years
the Ten Commandments
until I got the words
    perfect,
the whish of *w*,
the kih of *k*,
Sister Ann Zita standing
for the daily hour
in the auditorium's dark,
listening to a lisp so bad
she couldn't understand
a word I said, the belt
    a blur,
the bloody pad held
before my face,
boy looking up at a smile
    to my right,
a frown to my left,
masks, I'd learn later
    in life,
that people put on during
    plays,
father mask of rage,
mother mask of blood,

my lips forming beneath
    the repeating mask
for the black-winged nun
who clicked beads
and murmured prayers
while I went on and on,
Thou Shalt,
Thou Shalt Not,
teaching me sin,
teaching me how to say it.

Anointing Her Five Senses

Each morning she'd drop
a Milky Way or Three Musketeers,
with some piece of fruit,
apple, plum, peach, pear,
the twenty feet between
us nothing but blue air
as we'd both wait to see
if I'd catch what was tossed,
    not missing once,
as I remember it, reaching out,
sure, even now, when the priest
    asks,
Are there any sick in your
    house?
and dabs her head with the sign
    of the cross,
the last putting on of oil
for her sealed eyes and stitched lips,
for her ears that had curled
to every word I'd whispered up
those cool 6 A.M.'s just
above the rattle of cars down
    cobblestones,
a dab, too, for her nose
that could tell exactly
when the cake was done,
chocolate thick in layers
she'd wrapped in cellophane

just once for our most dangerous
        toss,
small cardboard plate
like a flying saucer that
        zagged
the air but never once
turned upside down,
shining there in my palm
like this chrism smudged
on the tip of her nose
with the priest's words
to heal the body and soul
        of the sick,
my eyes risen still
        to that window
where she would sit,
        my hands half-
lifted in that small room
        of her death
to catch, again, her morning
        gift.

For S.R., 1898–1973

Terrible Angels

When my son cries out
in Turku, Finland,
because he's lived
in a near-perpetual
dark for months now
and because five of
the kids at his school
act like wild dogs
as soon as he walks
through the doors,
I whisper the names
of the seven angels who
guarded me from the mother
with a belt, the silent
father with a beer,
I make the sign
of the cross over
my son's sleeping head
so he'll know the grace
of the Lord and the right
uppercut, so he'll know
not to take shit from anyone,
my fingers caught midstroke
when I call on Michael
with his sword, and Raguel,
who destroys with flames
of his tongue, my hand
suspended as I think of

my brother's rape,
my other brother's madness,
my father's last seven years
on piss-stained sheets,
calling on Uriel's twisting
serpent form even as I press
my fist down to my son's
hair-brushed forehead, feel
the terrible angels rushing in.

Part 3

The Long Ride Home

She wants to be thrown
in the field behind Belleview
Trailer Manor, where
she'd spent the happiest years
of her life, that's what
the will says as I fold
and unfold it again
in the car like a map,
keeping my eye on the road
the way she did
when my father would tailgate,
always too fast,
her feet stomping invisible
brakes while he let go
of the wheel
and lifted his hands
to light a smoke,
the dragon on his arm
shaking its tail
at her terrified face,
the lance through its heart
dripping blood
until she would break
and sob
and he'd stop
to get out and curse
wherever he was, traffic
sometimes piling up

behind us, blaring horns,
drivers' shouts,
my father's fists waving back
until someone swung,
then the long drive home,
tire hum,
radio on with some song
whose words I couldn't make out,
the three of us dead
silent in that car
more than forty years ago,
counting the telephone poles
to ourselves, sixty-six,
one hundred twelve,
all of it going by in a blur,
a jar of ashes, a jar of bones,
until we were home.

Thinning the Walnuts

Thinning the walnuts from the stone row,
    leaving them spaced
twenty feet apart, as the book says, so
    their branches
can spread, I cut what seems to be a
    mulberry
and the stink of shit fills the air,
reminding me of my father's last year
when he could not make it to the toilet,
his brown streaks across the linoleum
I would go down on my knees behind
with rags to wipe up, the stench
of his stealing and whoring and
    drunkenness
in the half-solid, half-liquid mass,
the peanuts he gulped at Boney's Bar
    making me gag,
the yellow tint a hint of my mother's
    leaving
in the tight black dress with fake
    pearl necklace,
fake pearl earrings, streaks of black
for his Guam and Guadalcanal,
his dead brother, his dead son,
the malarial fevers broken in a green tub,
the black holes of his face absorbing
    the little light

left in that rowhouse kitchen, the dark-
        ness of him
smeared on that floor he crawled across,
        I know, on all fours
just hours before, cursing God between
        his racking
coughs, cursing the bitch, the morning
        light, the son
he called to upstairs, who would not
        come down.

Angels in the Experimental Catechism/Math Class

I could feel God slowing down, turning
    from pure
thought to light and finally to matter
    scarred
as my heart-filled desk, what was left
    of Him
filtering through the seraphim, cherubim,
    and thrones
and then through the second order, the third,
where my guardian angel kept his wings
    on my either side,
tried to stop me from staring at Karen
    Awlen's tanned
leg tucked under the gray plaid skirt,
tried to hold back my hand from Donna's
    gold hair
streaming across my desk each time she
    leaned back her head,
my breath steaming the air by the window
    where leaves
turned orange, yellow, red,
and the high school girls swayed in circles
    on the sidewalk,
one laughing, another tucking in her blouse,
    all of me gone till
Sister Ann Zita tapped my desk with the heavy
    pointer, called me back

to the flash cards of 7 x 11, 230 ÷ 10, re-
    minded us all
that numbers could prove the existence of God,
that two angels hovered that very second
    around each of
our unholy heads, that they could see into
    our quartered, blackened hearts,
her soft voice whispering five of us would
    not live to be thirty,
making me turn around to guess Jackie Foster, Al
    Aldon, and Donald Wilcox,
maybe Jimmy Charette and Alfred Bouchard,
and I raised my hand to ask the odds of all of us
    going to Hell,
counting the whacks as I leaned over Sister's
    desk,
counting the motes that rose from my corduroy
    pants,
the kind with yellow and pink and brilliant
    green specks
that glittered like stars even as Sister
    whacked,
bead-rattling, black-winged, beneath
    the loudly ticking clock.

Obedient

We lined up in single file
    along
the wall, waited to be told
if we should go out the door
    or remain and burn,
fitting punishment for sinners
    like us,
Sister had hissed,
bombs falling even as she spoke,
    I thought,
craving to duck under my desk,
to wrap my hands around my neck
    and tuck it in
the way I'd been taught, but
standing there, instead, obedient,
the way I stand today on this
ice-crusted hill in Wassergass,
    still
waiting for the word to go
    or stay,
my wife and son down there
in the white house, with our two
    cats, our dog, warm,
while I trudge these hills looking for
    I don't know what,
listening for a voice I've never heard,
    even a whistle, a moan,
each cell in me alert as it was

back in that third grade class,
watching the sparrows swerve,
picking up branches to smell
    the bark,
ready to jump at a moment's
    notice,
to stop, or turn, or fall down,
to do whatever I might be told.

The Stone

When I'd heard, years after
    his death,
that my father had wanted
    to be buried
with a stone in his mouth,
I could only nod, amazed
    again
at the mind of the man
who'd taught me the presidents
with bribes of beer bottle caps,
    taught me French
as we smeared peanut butter and
jelly sandwiches at the white
    countertop
despite the loss of the woman
who'd screamed from the dark bed,
imagining he'd wanted to stop
whistling and playing
the harmonica in death,
that he didn't want
the old curse words or lost words
    anymore,
that he'd somehow thought
the stone would block
    even more
his already blocked heart,
that it would stop, in death,

what he could not, in life,
     stop,
knowing, too, I'm sure,
     he would not
get this last request,
but instead be buried
     by the rules
he'd always struggled against,
     no stone
in a mouth stitched shut
with thick black thread.

God's Blessing

When Sister sent Joe
to the nurse's office,
we could hear his leg braces
    clatter
down the long green corridor,
the heavy door squeaked open,
    clicked shut,
Sister's voice reminding us
that God gave Joe polio to
    test
him, and to bless him, and I
    thought
of my father's jungle-rotted
    face,
my older brother's crossed
    eyes,
wondered what God had in store
    for me
now that we were all driven out
    of *Paradise,*
word Sister flung at us as she
    held up
the picture of Adam and Eve,
a big green snake coiled
in an apple tree just
like the one by Big John's fence
I planned to climb that very dusk,
when the shadows darkened

and no one could see me run,
bent, from tree to tree to knock
     down
the apples that were not mine,
     sweet,
delicious, juicy apples I'd eat
     in the backyard's
garbage shed, knowing it was a sin,
     cracking
the thick core open with my teeth
so I could get to the black shiny
     seeds.

The saints always

                              had their hands up
with a cupped world, a rosary, a quill,
     a sword,
God's finger always pointing at Adam
     and Eve,
at the snake, at me as I sat, slouched,
     in the last
seat of that fifth-grade class
     memorizing the Commandments,
     the Seven Deadly Sins,
     the Apostles' names,
picking out the one that fit me best,
     Thou Shalt Not Kill,
     Lust,
     Judas,
finding myself wherever I looked, the
     bad
thief hanging on his left-side cross,
the one who clubbed his brother to death,
who threw his brother in a pit,
who ran away and spent his last cent,
who had the devil cast out of his house
only to have him return seven times worse again,
Peter, gutless, denying Christ, me knowing
     I was adopted
no matter what they said, the black angel
there in my heart, my balls, my brain,
     wings spread wide,

carrying me off even as I chewed
warts on my hands, sucked the blood
because I was afraid to let it drop
    on the desk
where I had carved tits and cunts and *shit*
    and *fuck,*
knowing it would leave a stain
I'd never wipe away, the mark of sin
that Sister would be sure to see
    no matter
how many rosaries I prayed,
    no matter
how many correct answers I gave.

What Kind of Man

In twenty-seven days
my father will die again,
November second's morning
with black wings
ripping and lifting him
while his drunk girlfriend
runs into the cobblestoned street
yelling for help which comes too late,
and I'm here raking leaves
like the leaves on that street,
red, brown, green, gold,
with a son my age when my father died
jumping into my piles
and strewing the once-raked leaves
all over the lawn, making me yell,
Go ahead, right now,
pick them all up,
which he tries to do
in his starred corduroy pants
and white turtleneck,
jacket tossed onto the porch
where the dog's asleep on it,
his hands smaller than most of the leaves
that crinkle in his fingers
or fly away in an always unexpected wind,
and I try to understand what
kind of man would do this to his son

but see only the rake's
twenty-two long green claws
and the vast expanse of leaves fallen,
where my father's heart is hidden
and his drunk girlfriend is running wildly through them.

My son won't stop making

them,
snowmen of all sizes,
    one
a good five feet tall
    down
by the pond, a small
    one
by the garage, my son's
    gloves
on the snowboy's finger-
    less
hands, his Chicago
    Bulls
wool cap on the bald
    head,
and on the north side
    of
the barn, a snowwoman,
    two
snowballs smushed on as
    breasts,
gravel bits as nipples, a
    mop
for hair flowing over her
    pure
white shoulders, my son
    standing

there right now, finish-
    ing
her off, a black scarf,
    red
plastic circle for a
    heart,
long red plastic strips for
    lips
he suddenly leans forward to
    kiss
in the below-zero, howling
    wind.

Last night, between dusk and

dark,
I walked the upper fields
        trying
to see how well I could tell
        obstacles
in the black, the way I used
        to do
when I was a child back
on Olmstead Street and would
        sneak
up Big John's Hill
as soon as their voices started
        to rise,
when her lips began to quiver,
when he piled the columns
of coins into the leather
        purse
and gulped the Schaefer's.
By then I was well into
        what I thought
was a forest of birch, scrub
oak, poison sumac I'd rub
my hands across to feel
        the soft fuzz,
remembering my crazy Mohawk
        grandfather's
warning that the sumac's
        clumped

balls of poison would run
madly in the veins
of whoever dared touch
    it in the dark,
my eyes searching the sky
    for a hint of gray,
no reprieve for me, I knew
    even at seven,
when I grasped the slender
trunks and began to sway.

Part 4

In the Mind of God

When Sister hissed, *We are always*
        in the mind of God
in that fifth-grade class, I looked
around to see if everyone else
        believed it,
only Joey McGraw winking back,
passing me the sketch of a prick
on blue construction paper,
me passing him back one of a cunt,
in the mind of God scribbled
across the bottom with hair-like
        strokes,
then the pigeon taking a crap
on the window ledge of city hall,
the Freihofer horse taking a crap
on the cobblestoned street,
the two of us outdoing ourselves
with outlined rats and cats turning
        on spits,
my father reeling out of Boney's Bar,
his sister lying down, legs spread, in
        the back seat of a car,
snakes and knives and devils' horns
drawn that long afternoon as rain
turned to sleet and the world
        darkened
as it does right now outside my window,
Sister long dead, and three others

from that class that I know of,
cancer, heart attack, a leap
from the Black Bridge between Cohoes
    and Watervliet,
all of them *in the mind of God,*
with my son's learning disabilities
from being hit by the speeding
Buick on Wassergass Street,
and my older brother's death in madness,
even the biblical sparrow right now
    perched
precariously on a windy branch
outside my window, staring in
at me while I stare out, a stupid
sparrow, I whisper, to still
be this far north in late November,
a fucking dumb sparrow not to have
    flown south,
cursing him for refusing to leave
with his small beads of eyes,
his orange-yellow beak,
the tiny claws that cling to the branch
    no matter what.

Nailing in New Braces

Within ten years, probably,
my old friend, who is like
a father to me, will be
dead, and my wife's father,
too, and my mother, in her
trailer of Belleview Manor,
and a whole list appears
in my head, a roll of paper
that keeps unwinding—
that's what I'm thinking as
I stand on the second top-
most ladder rung in a below-
zero wind to nail new braces
under the gutter that has
collapsed with the excessive
ice that's gathered this
winter, one eye on the thin
slate of the barn roof the
ladder rests against, the
other trying to align holes
in the braces with new wood,
wishing now I had brought up
some good inch-and-a-half
brass screws and the cordless,
or at least the self-sealing
nails instead of these eight-
pennies, the sun half-set
beyond the hill, one huge

blue-red cloud-wing spanned
across the ridge that lifts
the entire field of white
and blue spruce, the barn, the
pond and chicken coop, with me,
     up into it.

The Burning Hours

I'd sit for burning hours
 in the kitchen
with the cool washcloth
 on my forehead,
thinking of the enema
we'd eventually get to
on the bathroom floor,
 the cleansing,
as my mother called it,
then the pillow on the couch,
 the book, the blanket,
how they would not shout
that night because I was sick
 upstairs
with a bad fever, him counting
 his coins
and sipping beer, her scrubbing
her hands red in too-hot water
to get all the germs off the glasses
 and dishes,
holding each spoon, knife, and fork
to that dim Olmstead Street light
before setting them into the tray,
 one
of their quiet footsteps on the stairs,
the door creak, the light felt
 through closed lids,
the darkness again and that one's
 descent,

the most I knew of their love then,
    now, father dead,
mother in madness, what's left—
the quietness of the knob turned,
    the looking in
I did not dare open my eyes to see,
the utter dark with the door's closing
    click
that seeped in and set me free.

Taking Inventory as She Weeds

The pond's up, water swirling
    smoothly
into the overflow pipe,
my wife wants to make love
just about every third night,
every Sunday when Josh
gets to go with his sister
    to the movies,
woodpile high with splits
waiting to be stacked,
not one chip or crack
    in the paint
I spent twenty-one days
    last May
putting on the house,
although it was a hard winter,
those long nights of her
    tossing
on the far side of our bed,
names mumbled I could not
    make out,
sometimes shouts, flailing legs
    and arms
until I wrapped her hard
and whispered it was all right,
    not knowing then
what I was talking about,
not sure even now

although the bad dreams
seem to have stopped,
her lips no longer cracked
        and bitten,
her voice softer as she limps
from tulips to lilac to daffodils
in the turning garden,
thrusting the long forked tool
for the root of weed
she holds up like a trophy
        for me to see
in the sudden April wind.

Any Place, Any Time

I lug the oxygen tank
up the fourteen steps
behind my brother's gasps,
into the room where brass
pots and pans hang
from every wall, reflect
the two of us back,
a strange gold-orange-yellow,
from every possible angle—
the tank lighter than I thought
it would be, smaller,
the hiss into his tube a whisper
like those nights he'd play
Santo and Johnny's guitar love songs,
"Sleepwalk" circling in that dark parlor
until we both slept and woke to this,
him drowning in his own phlegm,
our mother downstairs
frying eggs in gobs
of sizzling butter, with ham
and sausage off to the side,
yelling up, "Come down
soon or it'll all get cold."

He shows me the picture of him and Bunny,
tells me he loved her despite
the fact that she loved Jack Pyskadlo,
despite his two marriages and three kids,

reminds me Santo and Johnny
played for them while they made out
and he felt her breasts and breathed
her soul into his so they could never part,
although I can barely repeat it,
her soul, his soul, all of that
so hard to believe some nights
it's the most I can do to beg The Great Invisible
to let my son live a long and healthy life,
take me instead, any place, any time,
as we used to say when some kid
wanted to pick a fight,
Yeah, any place, any time,
our small fists clenched with the thumb outside
so it wouldn't break when we swung
with such tremendous force
the four columns of the world
would fall before us,
the armies of fire and of storm bow down,
and we would walk into the glass-littered
alley to punch and be punched, blood
flowing as it always does, our blood,
onto clean shirts and pants and shoes,
but mostly in big, splashing drops
onto the ever-thirsty ground.

For Paul Martin

Doing the Laundry

Having mastered the wool,
the cotton, the linen
cycles, then permanent
press and delicate,
I dance
in the laundry room
when you're gone
off to work, our
son in school,
sorting the lights
from the darks
so they will not
run, just enough
bleach to remove
the stains from
the whites, I
whirl
to the spin cycle's
beat, lightly hum
to the dryer's roll,
bringing down
the three wicker baskets
from the three closets
of clothes,
singing a song
on the stairs
where the brass angel
stands and guards

our house, my thumb
rubbed across her face
and down her wings
no matter how full
my hands are,
no matter if I drop
a sock, a shirt, a bra,
wanting to kiss her lips
but finally knowing better
than to go too far,
suspended there a moment
with love overspilling my arms.

Noon, Wednesday in Wassergass

with snow
swirling the air so thick
I cannot hear my son,
who's waving his arms
over by the barn,
his mouth moving but
no words coming through,
just the swish of flakes
and wind down the hill,
just the snow devils whirling
from the barn roof that swoop
as though to carry him off
the way the black wings
settled on my father's chest
one Sunday morning and lifted
      him,
or so his girlfriend said
in her drunken whisper
the day of the wake,
barely able to stand, lipstick
      smeared
on her chin, leaning her breasts
into me as I backed away,
the thought of fucking her there,
then gone, here, now, for another
      moment
as I walk toward my son to hear
what he's shouting into this storm,

smelling her old perfume and beer
    breath
all over me, the give of her tits
against my white-shirted chest,
the slight scratch of her stiff
hair against my cheek as I bend
to lift my boy into whitening air.

A shoe in the road, autumn's

first leaf here in Wassergass,
and my son asks in his small
voice, *Where, Why, Whose?*
to the drum roll
of a gold-red sun that's
richer than the fresh cold
we open our windows to,
my shaking head
and shrugging shoulders
not good enough
as he looks back
to watch it lie there, still,
on the yellow line
of the curve,
Like a dead squirrel,
he offers, trying
to help,
or a groundhog,
a chipmunk, a skunk,
a litany of the dead
he's seen on this ride
back and forth to school
where they don't talk of
what he's already sensed,
a shoe with a missing foot
something to be reckoned with,
and the hands that laced it up,
and the brains and the eyes and the heart.

Ripping slate off the barn roof,

      fifty
feet up in cold Pennsylvania
      February,
I think again of my fat friend
Jeannine, dead just three days ago,
      failure
of a congestive heart, the voice said
over long-distance telephone,
too much weight carried those nights
on Olmstead Street when the boys
      came 'round,
her lips red, cheeks red, French
      songs
easy in the dark by the canal
black leather jackets who tossed
me Tootsie Rolls and lemon drops
      to get lost
while they took her for a ride
around town in big-winged DeSotos,
fast-idling Fords, once a red
      Cadillac
with Elvis blaring "Jailhouse Rock"
      as she hopped
in with a laugh, told me not to
      move off
the porch till she got back, me
      saying *OK*,

OK, which I find myself repeating
        today,
up here where no one can hear
except a few scruffy sparrows too
        stupid to fly south,
the cold of the slate seeping into
        my gloves
telling me I'll soon have to go
        down
the chicken ladder, slow, so the
        blood
will come back into my cramped legs,
        and I won't
miss the ladder's top rung, the tricky
        part,
I know, that first step off into air,
feeling around for something, anything,
        to hold me up.

She Returns for the
Last Putting On of Oil

While the priest made small
signs of the cross
on the dead man's eyes
and lips, his ears, nose,
hands, and feet, intoning
Is there a man sick among you?
my mother was in the laundry
separating lights from darks,
she was ironing his one white shirt,
setting aside the paisley
tie and gold-arrowed tie clip
with the three rolling *R*'s,
she was matching the work socks
and folding the white sweatshirt,
shaking her head at the shit
stains on his shorts, the piss stains
she could not get out
with a full cup of Clorox
that peeled layers of skin
from her scouring hands
while I, with bent head, listened
to every thump of the iron
and click of hanger on that metal rod,
my ears tuned to the washing cycle
turned to rinse then spin, the
     imbalance
of the dryer my father had tried
often to fix that made it walk

into the wall as though drunk,
like him those nights he staggered
home from Boney's Bar, each
bump making my head jerk
before settling back
to the *Amen* and *Pray for us,*
the dabs of oil aglow
with prismed rainbows
on the dead man's skin I knew
she would soon enough scrub off.

Part 5

Rain Wash

Last night's rush of rain filled
    in seconds
the gutter and spilled, waterfall
    from roof
for over half an hour, Josh and I
    grabbing
soap cakes and washcloths, hopping
out from the porch into cool June
    evening downpour
to wash our naked selves, his fore-
skin slid back only when turned
    away,
growing up, eight, a young man
    with straight
shoulders, lean, curved arms and
    legs,
concave of buttocks shadowed un-
    der
eaves and maple leaves swirling
    down
in thunder-wind, lathering each
    other's
faces, necks, feel his long, thin
    muscles,
his heart beating fast as raindrops
    against
smooth chest, tanned body wriggling
    on concrete walk,

looking up, eyes closed, to catch
    torrent
in mouth, spit it out
at his father who opens, too,
lips,
    tongue,
        teeth,
            throat,
a pool of green June here
    in Wassergass,
where we wash ourselves.

Elmer

It was heavier than I'd thought
when I grasped the brass handles
and hoisted his dead weight up
in the solid walnut coffin that
cost more than he'd ever earned
in a good six months, the five
others groaning, too, as we walked
him a last time down the aisle

where he was known to soft-shoe
on his way to taking the Host,
something else to joke about
after, with the small sandwiches
of roast beef cut from one
of his own cows, and the strong
coffee with biscuits to drag
it down,
        like the time he'd
said he knew his head
was too full of thoughts when
the news of the tumor broke
and he laughed all the way
to the tires, where he stood
and waited for the wind to
flatten out so he could torch
them and not be caught by the law,

clever among the harrows and combines,
the old Ford tractors he knew

every part of, the original
and *antique* cost, he'd wink at us
when another stranger appeared
at his cold door to find all
six feet four of him straightened
up like one of the hills down back

where he'd always go after the money
was dealt and left lying on the table,
checking the winch or another few rusted
bolts to cut off, his welder's arc visible
all the way up to the house where we'd
look now and then from window to window
at the man down there working till
the air darkened and the flame went out.

Working Blacktop, 1963

Old Leo would bend to sight
his one good eye down along
    the taut line,
grumbling through spittle
to move left, move right,
to move back, forward,
to stand perfectly still,
perfectly rolled off
with a blub of tobacco
he slurped back in for another
    chew.
One hundred degrees
and the wheelbarrow waited
with its steaming blacktop
    and greasy fumes
while I stood in sizzling shoes,
not moving an inch, breathing slow,
    until he rose
with that aggie-sized cataracted eye
and said, *Done, now get back to work.*

Blueberry, Froggy, Frenchie, Canuck,
that's what they called us
as we paved their driveways and sidewalks,
wives in bathrobes looking on,
bringing the cold glasses out on trays
we were afraid to touch, smeared
as our hands were with the long day's work,

some of them in rollers, some
standing around longer
than was good for any of us,
especially Blackie who'd been
to jail twice already and would face
a long third term.
                        That was the year
I learned a man's work
drove men into the hard ground
of upstate New York,
the year Kennedy's head was blown apart
and grown men like Sam and Armand
hunkered on the truck's rails
and wept quietly into their
blackening hands. It was the year
I walked home all those dusks
with the day's fumes hung
on me like stinking ghosts,
brother ghost although
he would not drown on his own
phlegm for another seven years,
mother ghost although she'd outlive
husband, lover, two sons to find herself
lost in the Burnside Elderly Home
with a Shih Tzu whose name she forgot
and remembered and forgot.

Who could tell me as I pick-
axed cracked walks up
to haul into the barrow
that my teeth would yellow
like an old dog's,
that my daughter would grow stranger
than any woman I'd pass on the street,
that one son would look for himself
for three years and not find anything?

When Old Leo died I didn't
go back for the funeral
although I heard his brother,
Armand, was there and coughed
blood in the middle of the sermon,
and that Ziggy and Blackie and Porky
were pallbearers, all
on one side of the coffin,
that when they lifted it up
the whole church shifted for a moment,
they were still that strong.

The Flying Monk in Flames

When Father Tousignant came to talk
        about the Flying Monk,
St. Joseph of Cupertino, all the kids
        in the class laughed,
but I hung onto my desk, thought
of those nights I rose above
my bed and soared over woods and fields,
the times I flew near the sun and looked
back to see rainbow sheen on black, oily
        feathers.
Staring at the saint who floated
above a crowd of believers
pointing up, I felt myself lift
a few inches inside my body,
whispered God to let me stay heavy,
to let me settle back into what I
        thought was myself,
no way of knowing then I would wake
one day to such weight, a lump
of lasagna I ate for dinner last
night, the french toast this morning,
no way of knowing I would not
even be able to rise a few feet
from the earth in my dreams
where my wife walks away with
        another man
and I rage for broken arms and legs,
where my first love comes back,

both breasts sliced off,
even that not being enough
    for the cancer
that rose through her spine
into her neck, her head,
until she was gone like the monk
    into the fire of time,
only part of his robe and bare feet left
    as he rose
above the candled trees with flames
    that leapt
onto his knees and encircled his waist,
only one arm and hand with unconsumed
    flesh
free to finger the fiery beads
even as they devoured him.

Burning the Angels

He would twist the white
sticks into wings, a neck,
a head, a halo of felt
and then stick the tip
of his lit cigarette
to its feet, watch it
flare up, *Going to hell,*
he'd whisper when he
let it drop back
into the ashtray's
glass that first
blackened then cleared,
leaving a small pile
of ash and thin wire
strips too hot to touch,
some nights giving them
names as he gathered
them up, Marjorie
always first, then Ann
and Lorraine, one
with small breasts,
one with flowing hair,
all of their eyes nothing
but dots where pencil
points were stuck,
all of their lips
upturned and smiling
with red-crayoned

lipstick, my father
lining them along the
table for me to count,
to lift and feel
their weightlessness,
my father teaching me
the foot, the knee,
the ass, the back,
showing me the simple
twist to make the head
look up, the brush
of black ink where
the heart pumped,
the two of us bent
to our work in silence
till the match flared
and burned to our
oooos and aaaas
even as they went
up in smoke.

Planting Damascus Firs

My lower right back shooting
pain with each step I trudge
from hole to hole to set
the small Damascus firs
into the ground, digging
out the rocks and clumps
of hard dirt, setting them
in just as the directions
say, the highest root
an inch below the earth,
thinking of St. Paul knocked
from his ass by the hand
of God, thinking of my father
measuring the shot of whiskey
before gulping it down,
thinking of my son, thirteen,
who's starting to climb
the barn's walls, to rappel
from the cliff behind the
house, who's planning
to scale mountains
and do movie stunts,
Sister Ann Zita's words
coming to me clear
as the crows' caws
from the crooked branch
of the dead white oak,
You shall be driven

into the fields
to labor under the sun,
me looking around,
trying to figure
what I've done,
what unforgiven sin
come back to haunt
me from hole to hole
where I cut jagged circles
in and lift the sod,
peer down into what I hope
will not be hell.

The Rare Coin

I can't remember the year
or whether it was a one- or five- or ten-
cent coin, only that it was buried
in her drawer of white underwear,
down beneath the plain cotton panties
and stiff bras, and that I took it
to Casey's Corner Store for a bottle
of Royal Crown and what? a bag
of popcorn, a Hershey bar?
and that it was days before she knew
it was gone, when the howling
and wailing began,
and the belt's welts
before I confessed and we two walked
across Ontario to get it back,
my hand in her hand across the cobblestones,
dodging cars, dusk,
looking, even then I thought,
like a mother and son out for an evening walk,
she bending down her pink-rollered hair,
the boy listening hard to every word
she said, as though she were telling him
his future, pointing to it just in front of them,
where he stared, silent, straight ahead.

We Were Insects and Animals

Richie Freeman was a red stallion
snorting at his desk,
Ann Harding a sleek black cat
purring with her legs tucked up
under her gray and red-plaid skirt,
Richie Reese an armadillo
with his leg braces clanging around,
with his love of the cactus
he sat next to all day and wanted to take home.
Each member of that fifth-grade class
was a worm or hawk, a slug or sloth
as we bent to our desks and sniffed
the ink of fountain pens that leaked
and blobbed all over the neat white sheets
slowly filling with letters, then words,
then sentences like snakes
that coiled and struck at us
when we had to decline at the board—
a blackness so vast
with its dull white clouds
we all sensed it was the universe
we were trapped in, obscure,
small stars, a half-moon, a full moon,
cosmic winds sweeping
where the janitor had brushed his arc,
all of us contained there
within the words we put down,
wanting to chew leaves, or lie in the sun,

wanting to shit anytime, anywhere,
and walk away as though it had never happened,
never dreaming of what memory would do to us
or our parents, our teachers, our friends and lovers,
wanting only to rub against something soft, something hard,
to dissolve minerals in our stomachs,
to jump on ice that shattered and boomed,
to bare our teeth, shake our fists
even as we lined up alongside the far wall
and counted off, one through twenty-six,
saying our names aloud before quietly sitting down.

Thin Pages

Never quite sure when to stand
        or kneel or sit down,
I kept my eyes on Charles Legasse
        and Irene Tousignant,
the smart ones who could find their way
in the black missals we were handed
        when we entered church,
the red and yellow and white ribbons
        splayed
when I flipped from thin page to thin page
for the right thing to do, the proper
        response,
like today, sitting here reading,
        staring out the window
to watch the rain dimple the pond,
thinking about the snapping turtle
who bites chunks from the stomachs
        of my carp,
of the muskrats I've trapped and
        drowned,
of my wife who's lost weight
for the first time in ten years,
who now dyes her hair
and wears high heels to work,
who's starting to sing in the shower
        again
and have her nails pedicured,
just the other night a thin bracelet

of silver hearts jangling
        on her ankle
when she rolled me over and got on top
despite her arthritic neck and hip,
when she came three times instead
        of once,
then left to read alone in the parlor,
the pages I could hear rustling,
so methodical, so sure,
as they sliced the air.

Knots

I'm trying to remember
    the knots,
figure eight, bowline,
becket bend, my favorite,
I'm trying to see again
my father's brown hands in the mirror
as they twined the Duke of Windsor
    knot
until it was done and I was off
to the Pater Noster and the hereafter,
down Olmstead, then Ontario, past
    Boney's Bar
where he'd practiced the sheepshank
and fisherman's bend,
where he'd made the long splice
between the two ends of frayed rope
the night my mother high-heeled out,

that's what I'm thinking as my son
ascends the climbing wall of Cathedral Rock,
stained-glass saints still lifting
their staffs and rods, their cupped worlds
    and glinting swords
while he stretches carefully for whatever hold,
hands powdered and taped, twelve years old,
checking my figure eight before he slid
    into the harness,
checking my safety knot before he rose,

not believing I'd learned them all
        in my father's smoke,
not hearing the names as I repeated them,
refusing to follow the leader
up and down, down, then up again
        until it was done
and he was safely tied in
and ready to ascend,

like my old man, no doubt,
face down on the smooth, cool, walnut bar
where he'd fallen asleep and finally ceased
        to exist,
the knots coming undone with his every breath,
until he was nothing but miles of rope
and a pair of knowing hands

that are my hands letting out and bringing in
        my boy at the other end
of a rope that's knotted right,
cinched, taut, and holding the weight.

Illinois Poetry Series
Laurence Lieberman, Editor

History Is Your Own Heartbeat
Michael S. Harper (1971)

The Foreclosure
Richard Emil Braun (1972)

The Scrawny Sonnets and
Other Narratives
Robert Bagg (1973)

The Creation Frame
Phyllis Thompson (1973)

To All Appearances:
Poems New and Selected
Josephine Miles (1974)

The Black Hawk Songs
Michael Borich (1975)

Nightmare Begins Responsibility
Michael S. Harper (1975)

The Wichita Poems
Michael Van Walleghen (1975)

Images of Kin:
New and Selected Poems
Michael S. Harper (1977)

Poems of the Two Worlds
Frederick Morgan (1977)

Cumberland Station
Dave Smith (1977)

Tracking
Virginia R. Terris (1977)

Riversongs
Michael Anania (1978)

On Earth as It Is
Dan Masterson (1978)

Coming to Terms
Josephine Miles (1979)

Death Mother and Other Poems
Frederick Morgan (1979)

Goshawk, Antelope
Dave Smith (1979)

Local Men
James Whitehead (1979)

Searching the Drowned Man
Sydney Lea (1980)

With Akhmatova at the
Black Gates
Stephen Berg (1981)

Dream Flights
Dave Smith (1981)

More Trouble with the Obvious
Michael Van Walleghen (1981)

The American Book of the Dead
Jim Barnes (1982)

The Floating Candles
Sydney Lea (1982)

Northbook
Frederick Morgan (1982)

Collected Poems, 1930–83
Josephine Miles (1983)

The River Painter
Emily Grosholz (1984)

111

Healing Song for the Inner Ear
Michael S. Harper (1984)

The Passion of the
Right-Angled Man
T. R. Hummer (1984)

Dear John, Dear Coltrane
Michael S. Harper (1985)

Poems from the Sangamon
John Knoepfle (1985)

In It
Stephen Berg (1986)

The Ghosts of Who We Were
Phyllis Thompson (1986)

Moon in a Mason Jar
Robert Wrigley (1986)

Lower-Class Heresy
T. R. Hummer (1987)

Poems: New and Selected
Frederick Morgan (1987)

Furnace Harbor: A Rhapsody
of the North Country
Philip D. Church (1988)

Bad Girl, with Hawk
Nance Van Winckel (1988)

Blue Tango
Michael Van Walleghen (1989)

Eden
Dennis Schmitz (1989)

Waiting for Poppa at the
Smithtown Diner
Peter Serchuk (1990)

Great Blue
Brendan Galvin (1990)

What My Father Believed
Robert Wrigley (1991)

Something Grazes Our Hair
S. J. Marks (1991)

Walking the Blind Dog
G. E. Murray (1992)

The Sawdust War
Jim Barnes (1992)

The God of Indeterminacy
Sandra McPherson (1993)

Off-Season at the Edge of
the World
Debora Greger (1994)

Counting the Black Angels
Len Roberts (1994)

Oblivion
Stephen Berg (1995)

To Us, All Flowers Are Roses
Lorna Goodison (1995)

Honorable Amendments
Michael S. Harper (1995)

Points of Departure
Miller Williams (1995)

Dance Script with Electric
Ballerina
Alice Fulton (reissue, 1996)

To the Bone:
New and Selected Poems
Sydney Lea (1996)

Floating on Solitude
Dave Smith
(3-volume reissue, 1996)

Bruised Paradise
Kevin Stein (1996)

The Ways We Touch
Miller Williams (1997)

Walt Whitman Bathing
David Wagoner (1996)

The Rooster Mask
Henry Hart (1998)

Rough Cut
Thomas Swiss (1997)

The Trouble-Making Finch
Len Roberts (1998)

Paris
Jim Barnes (1997)

National Poetry Series

Eroding Witness
Nathaniel Mackey (1985)
Selected by Michael S. Harper

The Surface
Laura Mullen (1991)
Selected by C. K. Williams

Palladium
Alice Fulton (1986)
Selected by Mark Strand

The Dig
Lynn Emanuel (1992)
Selected by Gerald Stern

Cities in Motion
Sylvia Moss (1987)
Selected by Derek Walcott

My Alexandria
Mark Doty (1993)
Selected by Philip Levine

The Hand of God and a Few
Bright Flowers
William Olsen (1988)
Selected by David Wagoner

The High Road to Taos
Martin Edmunds (1994)
Selected by Donald Hall

Theater of Animals
Samn Stockwell (1995)
Selected by Louise Glück

The Great Bird of Love
Paul Zimmer (1989)
Selected by William Stafford

Stubborn
Roland Flint (1990)
Selected by Dave Smith

The Broken World
Marcus Cafagña (1996)
Selected by Yusef Komunyakaa

Nine Skies
A. V. Christie (1997)
Selected by Sandra McPherson

Local Men and *Domains*
James Whitehead (1987)

Her Soul beneath the Bone:
Women's Poetry on Breast Cancer
Edited by Leatrice Lifshitz (1988)

Days from a Dream Almanac
Dennis Tedlock (1990)

Working Classics:
Poems on Industrial Life
Edited by Peter Oresick and
Nicholas Coles (1990)

Hummers, Knucklers, and Slow
Curves: Contemporary Baseball
Poems
Edited by Don Johnson (1991)

The Double Reckoning of
Christopher Columbus
Barbara Helfgott Hyett (1992)

Selected Poems
Jean Garrigue (1992)

New and Selected Poems, 1962–92
Laurence Lieberman (1993)

The Dig and *Hotel Fiesta*
Lynn Emanuel (1994)

For a Living: The Poetry of Work
Edited by Nicholas Coles and Peter
Oresick (1995)

The Tracks We Leave:
Poems on Endangered Wildlife
of North America
Barbara Helfgott Hyett (1996)

Peasants Wake for Fellini's
Casanova and Other Poems
Andrea Zanzotto; edited and
translated by John P. Welle and
Ruth Feldman; drawings by
Federico Fellini and Augusto
Murer (1997)

Moon in a Mason Jar and
What My Father Believed
Robert Wrigley (1997)

The Wild Card:
Selected Poems, Early and Late
Karl Shapiro; edited by David
Ignatow and Stanley Kunitz
(1998)

UNIVERSITY OF ILLINOIS PRESS
1325 SOUTH OAK STREET
CHAMPAIGN, ILLINOIS 61820-6903
WWW.PRESS.UILLINOIS.EDU